T0365621

Order this book online at www.trafford.com
or email orders@trafford.com

Most Trafford titles are also available at major online book retailers.

 www.trafford.com

North America & international
toll-free: 844 688 6899 (USA & Canada)
fax: 812 355 4082

Our mission is to efficiently provide the world's finest, most comprehensive book publishing service, enabling every author to experience success. To find out how to publish your book, your way, and have it available worldwide, visit us online at www.trafford.com

Because of the dynamic nature of the Internet, any web addresses or links contained in this book may have changed since publication and may no longer be valid. The views expressed in this work are solely those of the author and do not necessarily reflect the views of the publisher, and the publisher hereby disclaims any responsibility for them.

ISBN: 978-1-4907-6635-5 (sc)
        978-1-4907-6634-8 (e)

Library of Congress Control Number: 2015917636

Print information available on the last page.

Trafford rev. 11/25/2011

THE Homeplace

BY SHARON KRAUS

PHOTOS BY SHARON KRAUS

The homeplace is an old family farm in the Midwest.
It has been farmed for over a hundred years. Several generations have lived and worked on
this farm since the late 1800's, when a home was first built and the land first farmed.
It is a delightful place, full of history and great stories.

The homeplace is a wonderful haven.
There are hills and valleys, big shade trees and lots of cows.

A long winding creek runs through the homeplace.
The spring fed creek keeps the water running clear and cool.

The cows drink from the creek and cool off in it on hot days.
They lazily graze the grass and lay in the sunshine.

All the animals like to come to the creek, the horses and other animals that live on the homeplace and the wild animals that make their homes here.
Deer drink at the creek and eat the grass.
They have their babies in the tall grass, where they are hidden and safe.

Herons, ducks, and geese all come to the creek to drink and eat.
Eagles fly overhead looking for mice and other prey.

The cats like the barns on the homeplace.
They love to hide and play and most of all look for mice.

A couple barns are used for cattle. They go in the barns for shelter and to eat.

Hay is stored above, in the hayloft for feeding in the winter.

Another barn is for calving and milking. This milk cow is a brown swiss. Her mother and grandmother were both milked on this same farm.

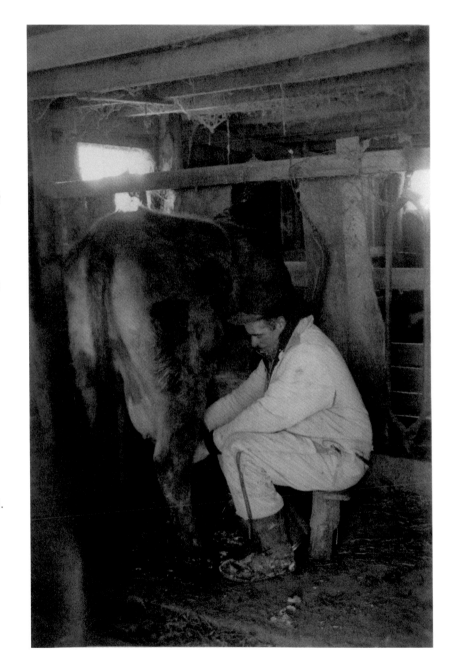

There is a barn for the horses.
Although, most of the time they would rather *be* outside.

There is another barn for the sheep. They come in for shelter at night and from bad weather. They have their lambs in the safety and warmth of the barn. When it gets warm enough outside, the wool is shorn from the sheep. It can be spun into yarn and made into almost anything.

But most of the time, they like to be out in the meadow.

A couple smaller buildings house the chickens.
There's one for the laying hens and another for raising chicks.

Chickens wander around the homeplace and peck at the ground for seeds and bugs.
They seem to carry on the conversations with their clucking and cooing.
Sometimes you can find pretty feathers on the ground.

There are bird feeders around the house at the homeplace.
They are kept full of birdseed in the winter when it's hard for birds to find food.
There are bird houses for them to make homes in
but most of them make their nests in the trees.

The Homeplace is sorrounded by wildlife.
Everywhere you look, nature gives interesting and amusing things to see.

One of the most exciting things to see is when baby animals are born.
They need help sometimes when they are small
or if there are more than the mother can feed.

If a cow is outside when she has her calf,
she goes off by herself to have her baby in the tall grass where it will be hidden.
If she leaves to eat or drink it is hard for anyone to find the calf,
but if you go in the direction the cow is looking, you can find her young calf.

Paul is the man who farms this land. There is a lot of work to do.
Animals have to be fed and cared for. Crops have to be planted and harvested.
Fences need to be fixed and equipment maintained.
There's lots of mowing and barn cleaning to be done.
But if you like animals and being outdoors and of you don't mind the mud and muck,
then you would like farming!

At different times of the year,
the cattle need to be moved from one pasture to another.
The horses always help a lot with that job.

Everyday, whether it's hot or cold,
Paul is at the homeplace,
a good shepard and steward of the land.

There always been a enormous garden at the homeplace.
Juicy red tomatoes and yellow squash blossoms bloom where squash will grow.
Onion and garlic blooms above plants growing in the ground.
Peas and beans, cucumbers and pumpkins, all grow in the garden.

In the orchards, the trees bloom delicate flowers that turn into delicious fruit.

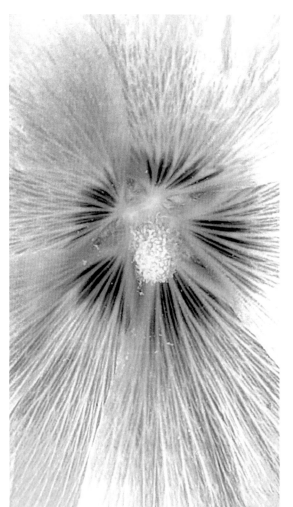

An old farmstead wouldn't be the same without some hollyhocks, zinnias,
lilies and bleeding hearts. And somewhere there has to be lilacs and morning glories.
The honeysuckle and honey locust trees perfume the air.

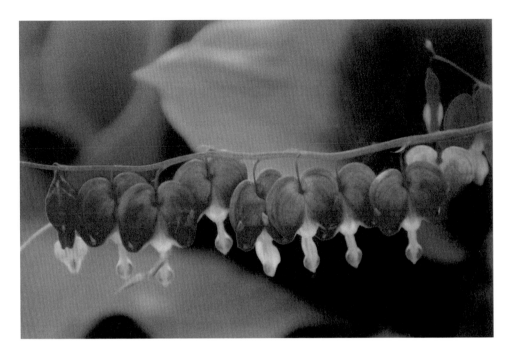

In the woods the ferns unfold their fronds when the breeze blows,
they look like they are dancing.
Wild flowers, violets, wild strawberries, roses and goldenrod,
all open their blooms for the sun.

And if that's not enough color, the sky gives beautiful sunrises and sunsets to the homeplace.

And Rainbows.

Printed in the United States
By Bookmasters